To Len. —JM

Arctic

Tales from the Lives of Inuit Artists

Adventures

Raquel Rivera

Pictures by Jirina Marton

GROUNDWOOD BOOKS
HOUSE OF ANANSI PRESS
TORONTO   BERKELEY

Contents

Pudlo and Kapik Go Hunting

One day Pudlo took his nephew Kapik out hunting for seal.

The sun stayed out longer and longer each day now. The weather was fine and the ice was breaking up. Kapik helped his uncle load up the kamotiq and harness the dog team. When summer came, Pudlo would use his kayak to hunt seal and walrus. But for now, he and Kapik needed the dogs to take them to the hunting grounds on the sea ice.

Together they set off. Like all hunters, Pudlo made different sounds to guide the dogs on their journey. One sound meant turn right, another turn left. Other sounds meant speed up or stop.

Dogs were always a big help in hunting. In winter, they could find the seals' breathing holes in the ice under the snow. But they had to be kept back from the seal hole. They had to be kept quiet so the seal wouldn't know that a hunter was waiting up above, harpoon ready.

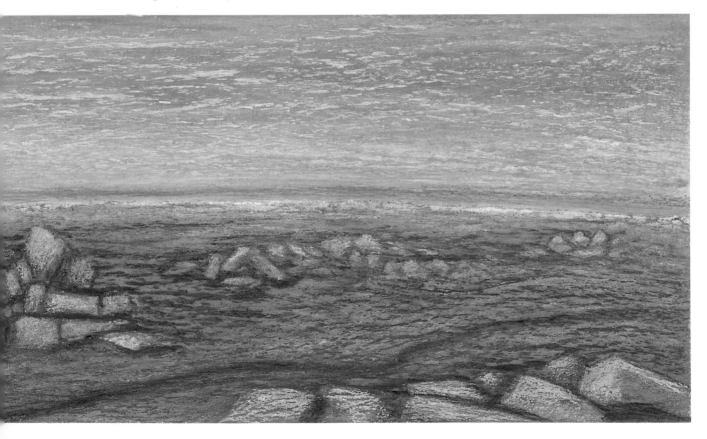

But now hunting was easier. Seals liked to crawl out of the newly formed cracks in the sea ice and bask in the sun. If Pudlo and Kapik were lucky, they would shoot many seals.

The dogs brought the hunter and the boy to the edge of the main floe where the ice was breaking up and melting into sea water. Pudlo and Kapik built an iglu for shelter. After some food and some sleep, they would try their luck at hunting. The evening was so clear that Pudlo left off the roof of the snow house so that he and Kapik could look up at the night sky.

But that night it started to snow. The snow blew in from land to sea. It blew into the roofless iglu and woke up Pudlo.

He lay awake for a little while. He listened to the sounds of spring — the cracking of the ice as it broke off the main floe and moved out on the water with the wind and the tide. He should get up. They were very near the open water. He didn't like the direction of the wind.

But it was hard to leave his warm sleeping bag.

Then Pudlo heard an especially loud BOOM! And a CRACK!

He leaped up to see what was happening. Normally, he would have had to crawl out of the iglu first, but this iglu had no roof.

"Kapik, wake up! Quickly!"

Pudlo looked toward the shore but instead he saw water. The ice under their camp had broken off and they were drifting out to sea. They had to move fast if they were going to get themselves back on land.

Pudlo led the way, choosing the spots where they could jump from one moving ice floe to the next one. Waves and currents jostled the floes, at times making them collide. Pudlo had to choose quickly but wisely. Falling into the icy water would be the end of them. Pudlo picked his way back to land, Kapik close behind.

But the ice shifted. The gaps widened. Kapik couldn't follow Pudlo over the last floe that led to safety, and Pudlo couldn't go back. Pudlo had to watch from shore as the boy turned and jumped his way back to the iglu, the dogs and the sled, all heading out to sea. Kapik grew smaller and smaller until he looked like a speck out there on the water.

If only Pudlo had his kayak with him on this hunting trip! He could have paddled out and fetched the boy right away.

There was no going back to camp. Camp was too far away, especially now that his dogs and kamotiq were lost to the ice. By the time Pudlo returned with help and a boat, who could say where Kapik might have drifted?

But at least he had his binoculars. He kept them carefully trained on the speck that was Kapik.

Pudlo thought a lot about ice. He watched it break off from the main floe in big pieces and wash away on the outgoing tide. He didn't like to see how it broke up into smaller and smaller chunks as it made its way out to sea.

At least if Kapik got thirsty he could melt some snow on the stove that was left behind. He could even drink tea and eat bannock in the floating camp.

Pudlo thought about how in the springtime ice that went out with the tide often drifted back when the tide rolled in.

A good hunter knows how to watch… and wait. Pudlo kept his binoculars trained on Kapik. He waited for the tide to turn.

Pudlo watched all day long. Finally, the water changed direction and slowly came back in.

Kapik seemed to be getting bigger. Was Pudlo imagining it? He lowered his binoculars. Could he see Kapik without them? Yes, Kapik's ice floe was drifting in!

Pudlo began running along the shore, trying to guess where Kapik might land. "Jump, boy!" Pudlo wished. "Start jumping from floe to floe. Bring yourself to shore."

But Kapik had other plans. He had gathered their things into a bundle. He was bringing in the dogs, too.

Kapik waited until a large floe approached, then he and the dogs moved onto it. Pudlo watched as the boy slowly picked the way for himself and the dog team. Pudlo wished he wouldn't. He wished Kapik would leave the dogs and just quickly get himself back.

Pudlo was grateful to see that the dogs knew their part. They knew to spread themselves out on the ice to keep their weight from breaking through it and drowning them all. He began to guide them from shore, calling out the commands they knew so well. Step by step, Kapik and the dogs made their way to a large ice floe that brought them safely to land.

What can a hunter say in the face of such happiness? A young boy drifts out to sea in an iglu… and returns! Sharp, fierce joy made Pudlo feel like they could live forever.

Pudlo Pudlat (1916–1992)

When Pudlo was a child, he liked to draw on the walls of his family's iglus, especially on the ice windows. But mothers discouraged their children from doing this.

"Don't carve up the wall," Pudlo's mother would tell him.

Pudlo didn't begin drawing on paper until the 1960s, when he was in his mid forties. He was living in a camp near Cape Dorset (Kinngait), the center of an arts program run by artist James Houston. Houston was one of

In the mid 1970s a studio was built for the artists in Cape Dorset, and Pudlo was able to work away from the noise of grandchildren and visitors at home. Later, when the other artists moved into a new studio, Pudlo was glad to continue working alone in the old one. When things were quiet, he explained, he could remember what he wanted to draw.

the first Canadians to appreciate the artistic and financial potential of carvings and images made by the Inuit.

Encouraged by Houston and his wife, Alma, Pudlo began to create drawings which

A Good Catch
Pudlo Pudlat
Color lithograph on wove paper, 1980,
Cape Dorset

In this humorous print Pudlo depicted everything a hunter needed to survive on the land: his strength, his dog and the appropriate tool for the job – in this case, a pronged fishing spear for catching arctic char.

could be made into prints. He had always hunted to provide for his family, but now he sold his artwork.

Pudlo's art often reflected his curiosity and his ideas about the changing world of the Arctic. He was the first Inuit artist to make a drawing of an airplane to sell to the public, and he is known for including planes, helicopters and power lines in his images. Between 1961 and 1989, he contributed as many as thirteen prints a year to the Cape Dorset graphics collection. By the time he died, Pudlo Pudlat had made as many as 4,500 drawings and 190 prints.

Kenojuak and the Goddess of the Sea

One sunny day in springtime, a hunter invited Kenojuak and her brother and sister to go for a ride on his kamotiq. He was going duck hunting. Did the children want to help look for ducks?

Did they ever! They all climbed onto his kamotiq and headed out to the floe edge. This was where the ducks could be found, diving for food and looking for mates.

The return of the water fowl was just one of the many gifts the ocean had in store for everyone in the warm season.

During spring and summer a whale might be spotted on the open water and chased into shore! Eating whale was a special treat.

The melting ice also meant that the arctic char were now swimming downriver to reach their summer feeding grounds in the sea. When they returned upstream, strong and fat, Kenojuak and her family would catch great numbers of them. Fresh char was delicious.

When summer came, Kenojuak would hunt for freshly laid eggs. She would also gather clams and salty seaweed from the water's edge.

The sea gave so many different kinds of food in the warm season, as long as the mild weather held, as long as there were animals to be caught. Kenojuak and her people counted on these things.

Riding along on the kamotiq to where the ducks gathered, Kenojuak looked out over the main floe. The sun glinted off the snow. Veins of shiny blue water snaked into the weaker parts of the floe edge. The sea was claiming back the ice.

Suddenly Kenojuak saw something swimming in the water, something unexpected. They all saw it and recognized it at once. It was Talelayu, Goddess of the Sea.

Talelayu ruled the seals, the walruses, the whales — all the sea animals. She lived at the bottom of the ocean. From there she would release the animals, so that they could swim to the surface of the water. Then the Inuit could catch them for food and clothing and heat.

It was important not to anger Talelayu. That was why hunters put a drink of water in the mouths of the seals they killed — a drink of fresh water, not salty. It was a good way to thank the goddess for releasing them, and to thank the seals for allowing themselves to be caught.

The hunter and the children gazed into the water. Talelayu's long dark hair flowed around her. It whirled in the currents she created with her strong fish-tail.

When the sea goddess became angry, bad things happened. She might send out a storm, making it impossible for people to travel or to hunt. Or worse, she might keep the animals with her at the bottom of the ocean, where no hunter would be able to find them. Then people would get cold and sick and starve. In desperate times like these, only a shaman could help.

Kenojuak's grandfather was a shaman with special powers. He could foresee the future. He could change into a walrus spirit. He could make himself invisible. He could even allow himself to be devoured by animals. A shaman who died and then came back to life was stronger than ever.

Kenojuak knew that her grandfather had met Talelayu. When the hunters couldn't find any animals, the old shaman made the dangerous journey to the bottom of the ocean, where all the animals surged in great hordes around the sea goddess.

Kenojuak's grandfather would then ask Talelayu the reason for her rage. Had the people up above offended her somehow? Perhaps they could correct their mistake? Sometimes the goddess was appeased if the shaman combed out the tangles in her long whirling hair.

But that sunny day on the ice edge, Kenojuak's shaman grand-father wasn't with them. Talelayu had shown herself to Kenojuak and the others — just some ordinary children and a hunter.

Never mind the duck hunt.

They turned the dogs around and headed for camp at full speed.

Kenojuak Ashevak (1927–)

Kenojuak grew up moving from one camp to another, learning from her grandmother how to use an ulu, how to prepare skins, how to keep the fire burning. When she was nineteen years old she married a hunter named Johnniebo and they started their own family, living the same way.

Kenojuak's family life was interrupted when she contracted tuberculosis and had to stay in a Quebec City hospital for three years. While she was away, both of her children died — one from food poisoning, the other from illness. When Kenojuak heard this, she wanted to give up herself. But her deceased father came to her in a dream, and she resolved to get better.

Kenojuak started making art in the late 1950s. Both she and Johnniebo were among the Inuit in the Cape Dorset area who were encouraged by James and Alma Houston to create art to be sold throughout North America and overseas.

Over the past forty years, Kenojuak has made drawings, prints and carvings. Her emphasis is on design, form and color rather than on illustrations of events or stories.

Kenojuak has been appointed a Companion of the Order of Canada and is a member of the Royal Canadian Academy of

Kenojuak once described the way she works as "just drawing as I am thinking, thinking as I am drawing." At the outset she doesn't have a plan of how a drawing should look when it is finished. Once she completes an image, a printmaker copies it using special inks and equipment such as stencils or a lithography stone. In this way many prints can be made from the original drawing.

Arts. She has received many other awards as well as honorary degrees from the University of Toronto and Queen's University. Her work is known and exhibited internationally. She lives in Cape Dorset (Kinngait), Baffin Island.

Spirits at Night
Kenojuak Ashevak
Lithograph, aluminum plate on paper, 1989, Cape Dorset

Before she created her animal figures for prints, Kenojuak would cut out animal designs from sealskin.
One day she was carrying a bag on which she had sewn a design of a rabbit eating seaweed. Artist
James Houston spotted the bag and asked Kenojuak if he could use the design to make a print. It was
the first of many prints and drawings to come. The print above is one of her later works.

Oonark's Arctic Adventure

Oonark sewed all the clothes for her family, right down to their furry socks. She used the skins of animals to make them. First she would lay a caribou skin out to dry. Then she would scrape it to make the stiffness go away. Then she would wet it a little, wait and then scrape it again and again. Finally, to make the skin really soft and supple, she would chew on it.

Oonark used her ulu to cut the skins. Skins with soft new fur were good for making shirts, trousers and socks. The fur was worn on the inside, all fuzzy and cozy. Strong fur from the autumn coats of caribou was good for wearing on the outside, just like the caribou did. Autumn fur protected Oonark and her family all winter long.

Oonark sewed mittens, trousers, parkas, amauti and the kami-it that kept their feet warm and dry. But she didn't just sew clothes. She also made tents, kayak skins, leads for the dog team — things she and her family needed to live on the land.

For a needle and thread Oonark knew how to use a sharp splinter of bone and a string of sinew from a caribou. But she preferred using a steel needle, which she could get when her family visited the Qallunaat trading post. Steel needles were stronger and they punched nice small holes through the skins.

There were many other things to buy at the trading post. Good things such as tobacco, flour, tea and — most important — bullets for her husband's rifle. Qallunaat had some wonderful inventions.

But Oonark knew that none of these inventions would be of any use if her family was not properly dressed for the cold. They say a hunter is only as good as the clothes his wife makes for him. Oonark's husband must never hunt wearing leaky boots. The seams of his parka and trousers must always be sewn with small stitches and kept in good repair. If the hunter freezes out on the land, who will return with the meat?

Oonark knew that the clothes she made were not only beautiful to look at, they were tools for survival — for herself, her husband and all of her children.

For many long winters and short summers Oonark looked after her family in this way as they followed the animals — hunting them, eating them, using their parts for clothing, tools and weapons. She grew from a young wife, just twelve years old, into a mother with many children and grandchildren, too.

But then one day Oonark's husband got very sick and he died.

While it is true that a hunter is only as good as the clothes his wife makes, it is equally true that a wife without a hunter is in deep trouble. Without the hunter there will be no meat — and no animal skins, no bones, no sinew.

Oonark had to think. How could she care for her young children? First they went to live with Oonark's mother and her stepfather. Then they moved to the camp where Oonark's grown son hunted with his uncle and his great-uncle. Everyone shared the food that the men caught, but without another hunter to provide for Oonark and her children, it was difficult.

This was not the only problem. The animals and fish had been scarce for too long now. The caribou had gone somewhere else and no one knew where to find them. Even families with plenty of hunters were having trouble getting enough food.

On top of this, Qallunaat were putting very low values on the fox pelts that hunters brought in from the land. It was becoming impossible for Oonark's people to trade for all the things they had become so accustomed to — the food, tobacco and bullets — all the wonderful inventions at the post.

More and more families from all over the Back River area began to make the long journey in off the land. They would seek help at the permanent village on the shores of Qamanittuaq, or Baker Lake.

Oonark's grown son gathered his family to do the same. Oonark still had a daughter and her youngest son with her. She sent her youngest off with her grown son. They would tell the RCMP that people were in danger of starving.

Meanwhile, Oonark and her daughter joined other relatives on their kamotiq. They would all try to get closer to Baker Lake. It was clear that it was dangerous to stay too far away.

But there was no food for the dogs and soon they became too feeble to pull the kamotiq with all its passengers. And so Oonark and her daughter got off. Their companions would go on and try to send back help. The two of them would just have to make do on their own.

They had an old stove with only a little bit of fuel for heat. They built a small iglu. They kept moving, looking for food and trying to keep warm.

Then a storm hit and blew hard. Oonark and her daughter were trapped inside their cold, dark iglu, unable to look for things to eat. There was nothing they could do but wait — and get weaker and weaker.

Finally, five days later, the storm let up. Oonark tried hunting ptarmigan. She tried fishing through the ice. But she didn't have much luck. Soon she didn't even have enough strength to cut through the ice. The end seemed very near.

Then one day they heard a buzzing sound in the distance. It

grew louder and louder. This noise wasn't like the boom of thunder. It wasn't like the whistling of the Northern Lights. It was the sound of an engine circling the sky. It was the sound of an RCAF plane landing.

They had been found! Oonark and her daughter would be going to Baker Lake after all.

Untitled
Jessie Oonark
Colored pencil and graphite, ca. 1976, Baker Lake

Usually the people in Oonark's art are occupied in traditional activities such as hunting or drying fish. But knowing something about Oonark's life, it is easy to imagine why she might have created this drawing.

Jessie Oonark (ca. 1906–1985)

Soon after their arrival in Baker Lake (Qamanittuaq) after being stranded on the tundra, Oonark arranged a marriage for her daughter. To support herself and her son, she took up work as a janitor.

Oonark (who added the name Jessie when she converted to Christianity) began to draw almost by accident. One day she was looking at the artwork of school children and said that she could do better. When Dr. Andrew Macpherson, a wildlife biologist, heard this he provided Oonark with drawing paper and some colored pencils.

Today Jessie Oonark is known around the world for her wall hangings and prints. She often developed motifs inspired by traditional Inuit decoration found in tattoos, hairstyles and clothing. In this way she has brought the cultural history of her people into her art.

Jessie Oonark started making art in her mid fifties and continued until illness limited the use of her hands nearly twenty years later. Her eight surviving children work as artists — drawing, printmaking, carving and creating wall hangings. During her career as an artist, Oonark was elected a member of the Royal Canadian Academy of Arts and was appointed an Officer of the Order of Canada. She died in 1985 and is commemorated by the Jessie Oonark Arts and Crafts Centre in Baker Lake.

When Oonark was a child, Inuit women would tattoo their arms and faces to look more beautiful. They would make their tattoo designs by scraping soot under their skin with sharp needles. When elders suggested that Oonark was old enough to receive her first tattoos, she refused. She agreed that tattoos looked nice, but she thought they were old-fashioned.

Lazarusie and the Polar Bears

Lazarusie was out walking one day when he met up with a polar bear.

It's bound to happen once in a while, especially when the sea ice is thawing or has melted altogether. That's when polar bears leave their hunting grounds way out on the water and search for food along the coastline.

Lazarusic was not out hunting bear that day, and Nanuq was not especially hunting man. They crossed paths by accident. Sometimes a rocky hill or a pressure ridge blocks a hunter's view. Sometimes sounds and smells are carried away by the wind.

Lazarusie was a good hunter and he knew a thing or two about polar bears. They looked big and heavy and lumbering. But they were quick. Lazarusie knew he couldn't just run away.

Dogs were very helpful when it came to polar bears. They could sense when a bear was approaching and howl a warning. If Lazarusie had been hunting Nanuq, the dogs would chase the bear down, nipping at his legs and darting away from his great bone-crushing paws. The dogs would yelp and bark, confusing and tiring Nanuq like no human hunter could. With dogs, a hunter had a good chance against a polar bear.

But that day Lazarusie had no dogs.

It was a stand-off between the Arctic's two top predators — Lazarusie with his rifle at his side, Nanuq with his teeth, his claws, his speed and his great strength. Neither of them wanted to turn away. It was too dangerous. But neither, it seemed, wanted to attack.

If Nanuq had been hungry enough, he would have leaped at Lazarusie, rifle or no. He would have ignored the blasts hitting him smack in the chest as he came down, crushing his prey. He would have used his last moments, tearing and walloping, to get at the food as best he could.

But humans are not a polar bear's preferred meal. They are too bony, not like a nice fat seal.

No, clearly Nanuq was not so hungry that day. He stood swinging his head from side to side — upset, wild and unpredictable.

Lazarusie waited. What should he do?

Nanuq watched Lazarusie.

Not like another polar bear Lazarusie once knew.

That time Lazarusie had been out on the land with a few other families. Nanuq charged right into the middle of camp, heading straight for a tent with a baby inside. He stood up on his hind legs and with his great paws and sharp claws began to tear the side of the tent. Lazarusie and the others shouted and threw things — rocks, tools, anything at hand — trying to scare him away. But Nanuq ignored them all. The sooner he tore through the tent, the sooner he could devour his prey.

There was one rifle in the camp, but its owner didn't want to use it. He needed a special hunting permit from the government to shoot at Nanuq. The permits were invented to help keep polar bears from becoming extinct. This hunter didn't want to go against the rules.

But Lazarusie couldn't allow Nanuq to harm the baby. The bear had to be stopped. He wrestled the rifle from the other

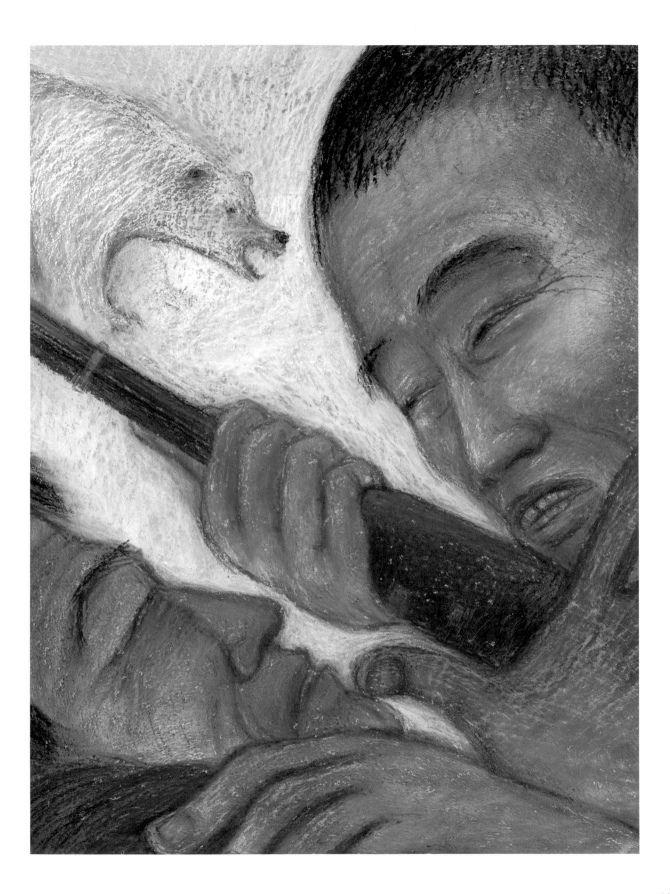

hunter and fired. Nanuq made an easy target standing upright against the tent. Just like that the bear slumped down — dead.

But today was another day.

Lazarusie was face to face with Nanuq again. He was grateful he had his own rifle with him.

Lazarusie raised his rifle. Nanuq continued to swing his head. Lazarusie took aim, very carefully. The bear did not back away. Lazarusie fired — BANG!

The bullet sped true to its target, blasting a ricochet of snow and ice chips against the side of the bear's face.

Nanuq turned his head to avoid the spray, and loped away.

Fantastic Flying Caribou
Lazarusie Ishulutak
Whalebone and antler, 1989, Pangnirtung

Inuit sculptors use materials from the land: stone, bone, antler, ivory and sinew. This sculpture was created using caribou antler and a vertebra from the spinal column of a small whale, likely a beluga or a narwhal.

Lazarusie Ishulutak (1948–)

Since the 1960s Lazarusie has made carvings from whalebone, antler and stone. His work has been exhibited across Canada and the United States and can be found in many collections. But Lazarusie has found the most satisfaction in his role as a hunter and provider. As a respected elder, he considers it important to pass on knowledge of traditional Inuit ways.

Lazarusie continued to hunt with his dog team when most others had taken up a snowmobile. When families began moving in off the land to settle permanently in Pangnirtung, Lazarusie and his wife and seven children were among the last to do so. They finally moved in the mid 1980s because his wife wanted the conveniences town life offered, and schooling for the children was a concern.

But Lazarusie keeps a traditional qammaq not far from the water's edge. He keeps meat on its cool front porch. Caribou sinew dries on a rack and sealskin trousers hang by the door. For interested visitors, Lazarusie will gladly light his qulliq and tell stories from the old days.

Today a few people still live out on the land around the Cumberland Sound, coming in to Pangnirtung for supplies every so often. But most Inuit spend much of the year in

When he hunted caribou, Lazarusie would walk out on the land for days. He returned with the heavy caribou on his back, already butchered and bundled within its own skin. It was such an ordeal that "you cry for the rest of the season," Lazarusie once joked with a journalist. "But you get a supply of food and the skins give you the warmth that lets you survive any weather."

town, going out on the land for stretches of several weeks at a time. For his own part, despite the comforts, Lazarusie Ishulutak remains unconvinced that life is better now than before.

Author's Note

The stories in *Arctic Adventures* are based on actual events in the lives of artists Pudlo Pudlat, Kenojuak Ashevak, Jessie Oonark and Lazarusie Ishulutak. For the most part, my sources were biographical accounts, art literature and cultural accounts of life in the Arctic.

The story "Pudlo and Kapik Go Hunting" is based on Pudlo's recollections as they appear in Marion E. Jackson's article, "Pudlo Pudlat: Looking Back," in *Pudlo: Thirty Years of Drawing* by Marie Routledge and Marion E. Jackson (Ottawa: National Gallery of Canada, 1990).

"Kenojuak and the Goddess of the Sea" is based on incidents and recollections in "The Autobiography of Kenojuak," as told to Patricia Ryan in *Kenojuak* by Jean Blodgett (Toronto: Firefly Books, 1985).

"Oonark's Arctic Adventure" is based on Marie Bouchard's article, "Jessie Oonark 1906-1985," in *Jessie Oonark: A Retrospective* by Jean Blodgett and Marie Bouchard (Winnipeg: Winnipeg Art Gallery, 1987).

"Lazarusie and the Polar Bears" is based on anecdotes related to me by Lazarusie Ishulutak. Elisapie Michael interpreted for us. Lazarusie's biography is drawn from John Roe's article in the *Kitchener Waterloo Record* (October 1, 1987).

My hope is that kids, parents and teachers alike enjoy reading these stories as much as I enjoyed researching and writing them.

Raquel Rivera
2007

Where the Stories Took Place

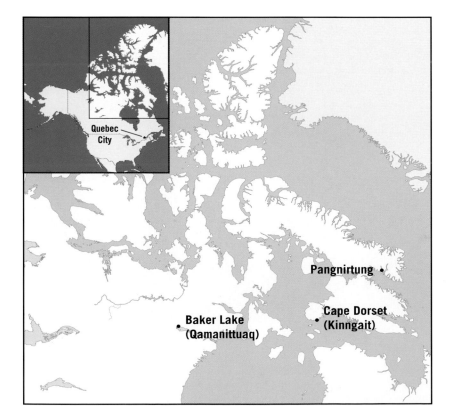

Glossary

There are a number of dialects of Inuktitut spoken across the Canadian Arctic. Even in the same area, spelling in the Roman alphabet varies with different attempts to correctly capture the sounds of the language. The Inuktitut words below are just one version of the many possible.

amautiq, amauti (pl.) – Woman's parka with hood for carrying babies.

bannock – Biscuit or pancake made with flour, water, salt or sugar, then fried in a little oil.

floe – Slab of ice on a body of water.

iglu – Snow house.

Inuk, Inuit (pl.) – Person who is a native of the Canadian Arctic.

kamik, kamiit (pl.) – Boot made from animal skins.

kamotiq – Sled made with slats of wood tied onto two runners. In the past, if wood was not available, animal skins were used. Bones were used for runners, or even skins doused with water and iced over.

kayak – Small, light sea craft, traditionally made of skin stretched over a wood frame, propelled with a double-bladed paddle.

lithograph – Print made by cutting an image onto a stone surface and inking the stone.

nanuq – Polar bear.

Northern Lights (aurora borealis) – Rays, bands and streamers of colored light that appear in the sky in the Northern Hemisphere.

pressure ridge – Jagged protrusion of ice made when sea ice cracks and crushes onto itself.

ptarmigan – Arctic grouse whose feathers turn white during the winter season.

Qallunaaq, Qallunaat (pl.)– Originally meant white person, now serves to describe all non-Inuits.

qammaq – Winterized tent built around a wood frame, insulated with moss and snow. Used as a more permanent winter house than an iglu.

qulliq – Dish-shaped lamp made from stone that burns animal fat for heat and light.

RCAF – Royal Canadian Air Force.

RCMP – Royal Canadian Mounted Police.

shaman – Person who acts as a medium between the natural and supernatural worlds, using magic to heal the sick, to predict the future and to control events.

Talelayu – One of many names, including Sedna, for the powerful goddess of the sea and its animals.

ulu – Crescent-shaped knife used by women, especially for scraping animal skins.

Further Reading

Ekoomiak, Norman. *Arctic Memories*. Toronto: NC Press Ltd., 1988.

Fleishner, Jennifer. *The Inuit, People of the Arctic*. Brookfield, Connecticut: The Millbrook Press, 1995.

Hoyt-Goldsmith, Diane. *Arctic Hunter*. New York: Holiday House, 1992.

Reynolds, Jan. *Frozen Land, Vanishing Cultures*. San Diego, New York: Harcourt Brace & Company, 1993.

Tookoome, Simon and Sheldon Oberman, *The Shaman's Nephew: A Life in the Far North*. Toronto: Stoddart Kids, 1999.

Wallace, Mary. *The Inuksuk Book*. Toronto: Owl Books, 1999.

Author's Acknowledgments

I'd like to thank the people of Pangnirtung, Baffin Island, for making my first trip to the Arctic such an incredible experience. Your generosity with your time, your knowledge and your humor were much appreciated by this Newbie-in-the-North. Thanks to Tommy Angnakak, Printmaking Cooperative; Ooleepeeka Arnaqaq, Angmarlik Interpretive Centre; Annie Bowkett, seamstress; Billy Etooangat, Parks Canada; Lazarusie Ishulutak, elder and artist; Bill Kilabuk, artist; Andrew Qappik, artist and printmaker; Juta Qaqqasiq, guide.

They say it takes a village to raise a child. Sometimes it takes a village to bring a book into the hands of readers. I am indebted to Kenojuak Ashevak, Lazarusie Ishulutak, Jessie Oonark and Pudlo Pudlat for their courageous and inspiring life work.

For their help in interpreting, fact-checking and their general support of the project, I'm grateful to William Noah of Baker Lake, Maggie Ishulutak of Pangnirtung, Leslie Boyd Ryan and Jimmy Manning of Dorset Fine Arts, and Kanayuk Bell and Pitseotuk Pudlat of Cape Dorset. The Conseil des arts et des lettres du Québec provided a grant toward the creation of these stories, making my trip to the North possible. And finally, many thanks to publisher Patsy Aldana, art director Michael Solomon, editor Nan Froman and all the other hardworking people at Groundwood Books, for putting this all together.

Picture Credits

14: B. Korda/Library and Archives Canada/PA 145608
15, 25: Reproduced with the permission of Dorset Fine Arts
24, 35: John Reeves
34: Photographed by Ernest Mayer, Winnipeg Art Gallery, from the collection of Robert and Irene Bilan. Reproduced with the permission of the Government of Nunavut.

44: Art Gallery of Ontario, Toronto (44.2x63x25cm). Gift of the Swinton Family, Winnipeg, 1994. Reproduced with the permission of Lazarusie Ishulutak.
45: Billy Etooangat, Parks Canada

Text copyright © 2007 by Raquel Rivera
Illustrations copyright © 2007 by Jirina Marton

Groundwood Books / House of Anansi Press
110 Spadina Avenue, Suite 801, Toronto, Ontario M5V 2K4
Distributed in the USA by Publishers Group West
1700 Fourth Street, Berkeley, CA 94710

We acknowledge for their financial support of our publishing program the Canada Council for the Arts, the Government of Canada through the Book Publishing Industry Development Program (BPIDP) and the Ontario Arts Council.

Library and Archives Canada Cataloging in Publication
Rivera, Raquel
Arctic adventures : tales from the lives of Inuit artists / by Raquel Rivera ; illustrated by Jirina Marton.
ISBN-13: 978-0-88899-714-2
ISBN-10: 0-88899-714-0 (bound)
1. Inuit–Canada–Juvenile literature. 2. Inuit artists–Canada–Biography–Juvenile literature. I. Marton, Jirina II. Title.
E99.E7R5758 2006   j305.897'12   C2006-902393-X

Design by Michael Solomon
Printed and bound in China

ONTARIO ARTS COUNCIL
CONSEIL DES ARTS DE L'ONTARIO

Conseil des arts et des lettres
Québec